Forensic Science

Peter Pentland and
Pennie Stoyles

CHELSEA HOUSE
PUBLISHERS
A Haights Cross Communications ✔ Company
Philadelphia

Chelsea House Publishers
1974 Sproul Road, Suite 400
Broomall, PA 19008-0914

The Chelsea House world wide web address is www.chelseahouse.com

Library of Congress Cataloging-in-Publication Data

Pentland, Peter.
    Forensic science / by Peter Pentland and Pennie Stoyles.
    p. cm. — (Science and scientists)

Includes index.
Summary: Surveys some of the scientific principles used in investigating crime scenes and suspects.

ISBN 0-7910-7010-7
1. Forensic sciences—Juvenile literature. 2. Criminal investigation—Juvenile literature.
[1. Forensic sciences. 2. Criminal investigation.] I. Stoyles, Pennie. II. Title.

HV8073.8 .P45 2003
363.25—dc21

                                                    2002001279

First published in 2002 by
MACMILLAN EDUCATION AUSTRALIA PTY LTD

627 Chapel Street, South Yarra, Australia, 3141
Copyright © Peter Pentland and Pennie Stoyles 2002
Copyright in photographs © individual photographers as credited

Edited by Sally Woollett
Text design by Nina Sanadze
Cover design by Nina Sanadze
Illustrations by Pat Kermode, Purple Rabbit Productions
Printed in China

Acknowledgements
Cover: DNA double helix, courtesy of Veronique Estiot/B.S.I.P./Auscape.

Kathie Atkinson/Auscape, p. 28 (bottom right); Veronique Estiot/B.S.I.P./Auscape, pp. 20–21 (bottom); Gunther/Explorer/Auscape, 25 (top left); Reg Morrison/Auscape, 17 (right); Ian Dadour, Forensic Science Unit, University of Western Australia, p. 28 (top left); Caroline de Koenig, p. 29; Joss Dimock, pp. 14–15 (bottom); Getty Images/Photodisc, pp. 24–25; Imageaddict.com, p. 8; Legend Images, pp. 26–27; Jiri Lochman/Lochman Transparencies, p. 28 (top right and bottom left); Steve Lovegrove, p. 25 (middle left and bottom); Terry Oakley/Picture Source, pp. 15 (top), 18–19, 26 (left); Red Cross Blood Bank, p. 18 (top); Victoria Forensic Science Centre, Victoria Police, pp. 4–5, 6–7, 9, 10–11, 16–17, 20 (top), 22, 23, 27 (top); Victorian Police Criminal Identification Squad – Melbourne, Australia, pp. 12, 13.

While every care has been taken to trace and acknowledge copyright the publisher tenders their apologies for any accidental infringement where copyright has proved untraceable.

Contents

Glossary words

When a word is printed in bold you can look up its meaning in the Glossary on page 31.

Science terms

When a word appears like this **dissolved** you can find out more about it in the science term box located nearby.

Have you ever wondered...

...how crimes are solved?

...if you would make a good witness?

Did you know that all the answers have something to do with science?

...how blood types are analyzed?

...how fingerprints are matched?

What is forensic science?

Forensic science is a term used to group together all the different sciences used to solve a crime.

The word *forensic* comes from the ancient Greek word *forum*, which means 'courts of law'. So, strictly speaking, forensic science is science to do with courts of law. Forensic scientists work with police and lawyers, and they use scientific processes to find and collect evidence, to identify bodies and to solve crimes.

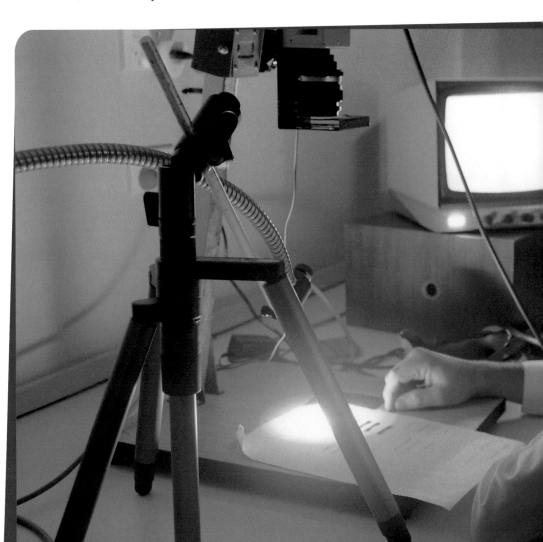

Scientists

Many different scientists work together to solve crimes. Serologists and chemists analyze blood types. Pathologists and toxicologists find out about possible causes of death. Police use scientific methods to collect and analyze evidence.

There are many types of scientists working to solve crimes, and they all have different jobs to do.

- Police investigate crimes and collect evidence.
- Photographers take photographs to record evidence.
- Forensic anatomists **reconstruct** faces.
- Serologists, chemists and biologists study blood.
- Toxicologists study poisons.
- Dentists study teeth.
- Forensic pathologists study how people die.
- Entomologists study insects.

In this book you will:

- find out how evidence is collected from the scene of a crime and how it is studied by forensic scientists
- see if you would make a good witness
- discover the science behind fingerprints, blood types, hair and fibers

- meet a forensic technician, whose work helps to solve crimes.

Have you ever read stories or seen a movie about people, such as Sherlock Holmes, who solve crimes? These people are very good at observing, asking questions and solving problems. They look for clues to help solve a crime.

A good crime investigator is always asking questions.

⊙ Was the event an accident or deliberate?

⊙ Who was the victim?

⊙ What exactly happened?

⊙ When did the crime happen?

⊙ Who else was involved?

⊙ Were there any witnesses?

⊙ What else can be found? (Things that may not seem important at first might turn out to be important clues at a later time.)

What is evidence?

All the clues gathered to help solve a crime are called evidence. When a crime is discovered, the area is sealed off from the public. Nothing is moved unless absolutely necessary. All details are written down, things are measured, diagrams are drawn and sometimes the scene is photographed. Descriptions from witnesses are also recorded. This process is called documenting evidence. Documenting evidence is important because investigators may not realize a particular piece of evidence is important until some time after the crime. So everything is kept, just in case.

Science fact

Leaving your mark

Whenever you go somewhere, you leave behind evidence that you were there. You might leave a footprint, a fingerprint or a strand of hair. You also take with you evidence such as fibers from the carpet. This kind of evidence tells crime investigators who has been where, and when.

Handling evidence

Forensic scientists must keep careful records when handling evidence. All pieces of evidence are carefully recorded and then stored. The date and time of discovery, the name of the person handling the item, and the method and place of storage are recorded. Whenever an item is handled again, these details are recorded again. If evidence is to be used in court, its location must be known at all times. It is important to know who has touched the evidence, when they touched it and why. Evidence that has been handled incorrectly or by unknown people may not be able to be used in court.

Matching evidence

When a part of something is left at a crime scene, it may be possible for the forensic scientists to match it with another part of the object. For example, if a torn piece of paper is found at the scene of a crime, and a suspect also has a torn piece of paper in his or her pocket, then these two pieces can be closely analyzed to see if they match. Matching of two halves of something is called fracture analysis.

There are other types of matching.

- Footprints can be matched to the shoes the person wore.
- Bullets can be matched to the guns that fired them.
- Fingerprints can be matched to people.

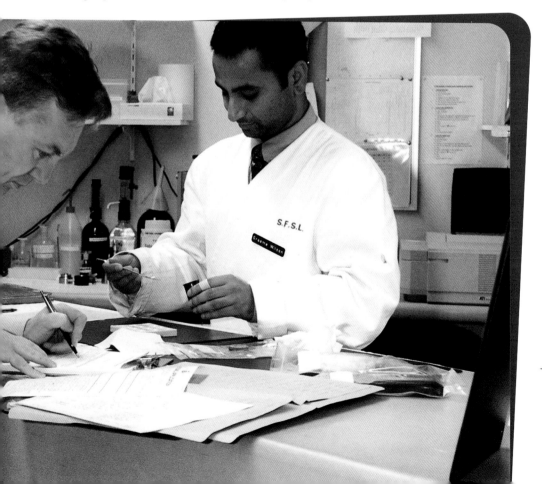

These scientists are carefully documenting evidence.

Have you ever taken a photo or used a tape measure or a magnifying glass? If you have, then you have used some of the tools that crime investigators and forensic scientists use. These tools, along with more complicated scientific instruments and computers, are used to help solve crimes.

Forensic scientists use simple tools such as a tape measure to help solve crimes.

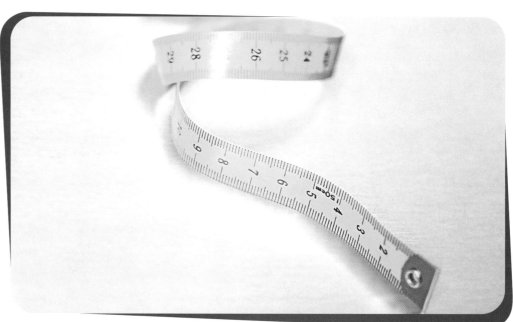

Measuring up

Police and forensic scientists use many different measuring tools. They use rulers and tape measures to record distances at the crime scene, such as the distance between footprints or the distance of evidence from a body. They use thermometers to help determine time of death.

Chemical clues

Sometimes it is difficult to tell what something is by just looking at it. Chemists can use a number of methods to identify smells and tiny traces of substances found at the crime scene. Mystery powders or liquids found at a crime scene can be identified. For example, if police suspect that a fire has been deliberately lit, they can use a method called gas chromatography to find out what chemical was used to start the fire. This method can also detect alcohol or drugs in blood and urine.

Invisible clues

Some clues are too small to be seen clearly. Good observation may involve finding clues that you cannot see. A clue could be a smell. For example, if you smelled gasoline at the scene of a fire, you would be suspicious. A clue can also be a sound.

Magnifying glasses

A magnifying glass may help to find clues like hair, tiny specks of blood or fibers from clothing. A magnifying glass is a glass lens. As light rays pass through the lens they are bent, which makes the image appear bigger than it really is. Magnifying glasses can magnify to different sizes, depending on the shape and size of the lens.

Microscopes

Microscopes are similar to magnifying glasses, but they contain two lenses. This means that their magnification is much greater. Microscopes can enlarge an object up to 1,500 times, so they can be used to see extremely small objects. One type of microscope that is often used by forensic scientists is a comparison microscope. This is like two microscopes in one. It is used for comparing and matching things like hair and fibers.

Electron microscopes

Electron microscopes use a beam of **electrons** instead of light to produce an image. They can magnify an object up to about 250,000 times. Electron microscopes are sometimes fitted with other probes to detect tiny traces of metals.

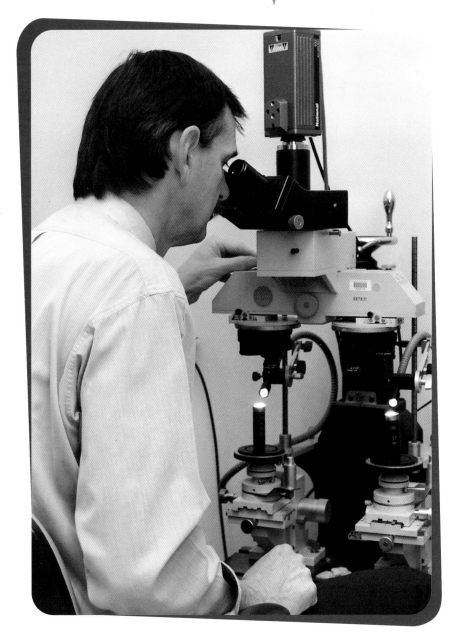

A comparison microscope allows the fine detail of two objects to be compared.

How good is your memory? Can you remember what you had for lunch yesterday? What about what you had for lunch 15 days ago? Can you remember the capital of Canada?

A witness is a person who sees or hears a crime happening. Good witnesses use their eyes, ears, nose, and memory. For police, an important part of solving any crime is talking to witnesses. Witnesses with good observation skills and good memories can help police to work out the order of events and to identify people involved in a crime.

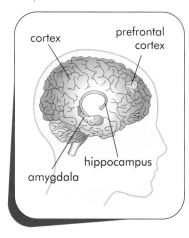

Several parts of the brain are involved in memory.

cortex

prefrontal cortex

hippocampus

amygdala

How does your memory work?

Memory involves using your senses—sight, smell, taste, touch and hearing—to send messages to your brain. Your brain processes this information into a memory.

At least four parts of the brain work together to 'make' a memory. These parts are the hippocampus, the prefrontal cortex, the cortex and the amygdala.

Different types of memory

There is more than one type of memory. Short-term memory deals with information you have just received. This memory is important if you are witnessing a crime. You often forget information stored in your short-term memory. If you write down the information and tell it to someone else, it may transfer to your long-term memory. Long-term memories build up over days, weeks or even years. Much of what you learn at school is remembered as a long-term memory. Recalling memories now and again helps you to remember them longer.

A good witness

When people witness a crime they are often frightened or upset. Their memory does not work in a straightforward way such as a video recording. Usually only bits and pieces of the event are remembered. When a witness is interviewed later, he or she has to piece together bits of memory to tell a story about what they saw and heard. You can be a better witness if you try to stay calm and concentrate on memorizing things like the color of a person's clothing or the license plate of a car. If it is safe, you can even try to write things down so that you can remember them later.

Try this

1 Work with a friend to test your memory. Ask them to put 10 or 12 different items on a tray, without showing you. Ask them to cover the items with a cloth.

2 Get your friend to take the cloth off for 10 seconds, while you look at the items and try to remember as many as possible.

3 When the tray is covered again, write down the names of as many things as you can. Then try to describe the things (their color, what they were made of, where they were on the tray and so on). Do you think you would make a good witness?

This witness is assisting a police officer.

11

Making faces

Can you remember and describe the sales clerk who helped you yesterday? Could you make an accurate drawing of this person, or recognize his or her face among a pile of photos?

Our brains seem to be particularly good at remembering human faces. We often remember faces without trying. Remembering a person's face can be a very important part of solving a crime. Making the memory into a picture is just as important.

Making pictures without computers

If a witness sees a suspect at the scene of a crime, they will describe the suspect to the police, who will then produce a picture of the face. Before computers, the picture could be created in a number of ways. At first the police used artists who were skilled at drawing portraits to sketch a likeness of the face of the suspect.

Later, the Identikit system was developed. Sketches of many different parts of the face were kept on file to help with the drawings. A type of nose, eye, ear, forehead or chin could be chosen from hundreds of sketches of facial features. These features could then be put together to form a face.

The next development was the Photofit system. This system used photographs of all the different face parts to make a 'cut-and-paste' photograph of the likeness of a person.

Before the computer age, hand-drawn and Photofit faces were used to create likenesses of suspects.

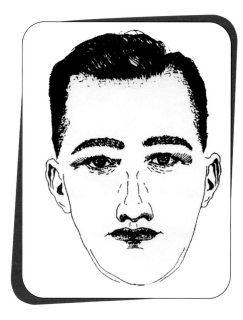

FACE

Computers are now used to make pictures. A police department and a computer graphics company developed a computer-based identification system for faces that was first used in 1989. It is called Facial Automated Composition and Editing system (or FACE).

Sitting in front of a computer, witnesses choose a hair style, chin shape, eyes, nose and mouth from a menu. Then they select hats, beards, mustaches and glasses.

The police graphic artists now start working to match other facial features such as skin color, freckles and wrinkles. The image now looks like a photograph.

These faces were made by a graphic artist using a computer.

Mug shots

Police take photos of known criminals. These photos are sometimes called 'mug shots'. (Mug is an old-fashioned slang word for your face.) Mug shots are stored in books or on computer files so that they can be shown to witnesses. The witnesses may recognize a criminal who was at the scene of a crime.

Forensic anatomists

When the remains of an unidentified person are discovered, a face can be reconstructed using modeling clay and careful measurements of skin depth. This job is done by scientists called forensic anatomists. This method has also been used to reconstruct faces of skulls found from ancient times.

Leaving your fingerprints

Pick up a small object like a paperclip or a pin. Now look at your fingertips. The sweat and oil on your fingertips as well as the tiny ridges on the surface of your skin help you to get a better grip. When you touch anything, the sweat, oils and **bacteria** leave a fingerprint pattern on the surface.

Unique patterns

Although there are four types of fingerprints, each person in the world has a unique set of prints. This means that there are no two identical fingerprints in the world. Even identical twins have slightly different fingerprints.

arch   loop

whorl   composite

There are four different types of fingerprint patterns.

Your fingerprints and toeprints begin to develop five months before you are born. Fingers and toes start off as stumps with bumps. As they grow, ridges and valleys form around the bumps. Each pattern of ridges and valleys depends on the size of the bump to start with. These ridges and valleys become our fingerprints. Throughout the 1900s, fingerprints were used as the most reliable form of evidence.

Famous scientist

Edward Henry

In the late 1800s, an Englishman, Sir Edward Henry, spent years examining and describing fingerprints. He found three different types of fingerprint patterns: an arch, a loop and a whorl. He also identified a fourth type called a composite, which combined features of the other three types.

Can you identify this fingerprint pattern?

Collecting fingerprints

If you dip your finger in paint, or your hands are dirty and then you touch something, you leave visible fingerprints. These are easy to see and can be photographed. If your hands are clean, the oils and bacteria on your skin still leave a fingerprint. These fingerprints are called latent fingerprints and are almost invisible. Police and forensic scientists carefully dust fine black powder over these fingerprints, so that they can be photographed for comparison with a suspect's fingerprints. It is possible to positively identify a person from just a small part of one fingerprint.

Some fingerprints must be dusted so that they can be seen properly.

Dactylography

The science of fingerprints is called dactylography. Today, fingerprint experts use computers to match fingerprints. This matching system plots onto a graph the points where lines in a fingerprint stop or where two lines meet. The computer can easily compare a plot of a fingerprint found at a crime scene to all the fingerprint plots in the computer's database. The Australian National Automated Fingerprint Identification System (NAFIS) is considered the best system available in the world. It is the only national computerized fingerprint system.

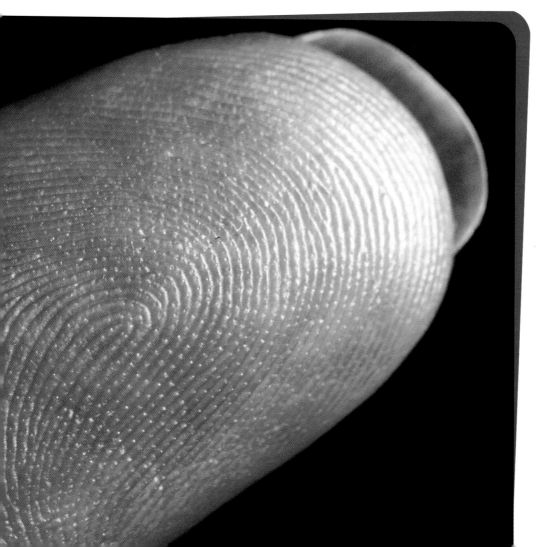

Weird science

American gangster John Dillinger went to amazing lengths to try to remove his fingerprints. First he had them removed by a plastic surgeon, but they grew back. Then he tried to burn them off with strong acid but they had grown back by the time he was caught.

Why are other prints useful?

Footprints

Whenever you walk on soft ground, or through something wet like mud, you leave a footprint. If you have shoes on, you leave a shoe print. These prints show the size of your feet and the make of your shoes. They can also provide information about your weight, height, likely age, the direction you took, how fast you were going and even if you were carrying something. At a crime scene, footprints can provide useful information about what happened, how many people were involved and the order of events.

The angle of the footprints and the distance between them are just as important as the footprints themselves.

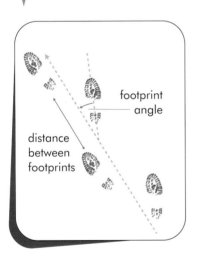

footprint angle

distance between footprints

Which way were you going?

If a straight line is drawn from the inside heel of one footprint to the inside heel of the next footprint, the direction of travel can be worked out. Each person has a characteristic foot angle. The distance apart of each print gives information about your height and how fast you were going. The depth of a footprint can also provide information about your speed and weight. For example, when you are running, your steps are farther apart and heavier.

Tire prints

Vehicles that were at a crime scene leave tire prints. The make of tire can be identified from the tread pattern. The wear on the tires and any marks such as nicks and other minor damage can help to identify the car to which the tires belong.

Your shoe size is not the only piece of information that your footprint gives away.

Casting prints

When shoes, feet or tires make a mark in soft ground, the mark is the 'negative' of the shoe, foot or tire. If you pour plaster of Paris into the impression, you can make a cast or reproduction of the print. Plaster of Paris is a powder. When you add water to it, a chemical reaction takes place and the mixture gives off heat. During the reaction, the mixture expands slightly so that the plaster is forced into the smallest places. The plaster sets very quickly, so you need to use it immediately after the water is added.

When you make a cast, features of the print such as depth, size, shape, tread pattern and any damage can be 'captured' in the plaster. The cast can then be taken back to the forensic laboratory for testing and comparing. It is evidence that can be stored long after the crime scene has been destroyed.

Science fact

Mysteries from the past

Dinosaur footprints can be analyzed like crime scene footprints. When dinosaurs walked in soft mud, they left prints that sometimes turned into fossils.

A meeting between one large meat-eating dinosaur and a group of smaller dinosaurs can be seen in the 'dinosaur trackways' at Lark Quarry in Queensland, Australia. There, a large dinosaur moved toward a group of more than 100 small dinosaurs. Moments later, the small dinosaurs ran in the opposite direction, their tiny footprints crossing the large footprints of the big dinosaur that had passed moments before.

The fossilized dinosaur footprints at Lark Quarry are a type of evidence.

17

Is all blood the same?

Do you know anyone who is a blood donor? Do you know anyone who has had an operation and needed a blood transfusion? There are many different blood types. You inherit your blood type from your parents and your grandparents. When a person gives blood, their blood type must be determined because the blood they donate can be given only to someone with a suitable type.

Blood types

In 1875, it was first realized that people have different blood types, but it was not until 1901 that Austrian biologist Karl Landsteiner was able to develop the most important blood grouping system, the ABO system. Today, blood typing is not only used for medical reasons. It can also be used to identify or clear victims and suspects in crimes.

The ABO blood system is made up of four different blood types. They are A, B, AB and O. The ABO system is not the only way we identify blood. There are many different blood grouping systems. The next most important system is the Rhesus system (the positive/negative system). Using this system, your blood is classified as Rh+ or Rh–. If you combine these two systems, you double the number of different blood types to eight. They are A+, A–, B+, B–, AB+, AB–, O+ and O–. Scientists have discovered other grouping systems. Using the systems in combination provides a more exact match.

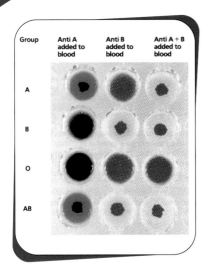

Adding antiserum to blood shows up different blood types. Different antiserums make the cells in different blood types clump together or clot.

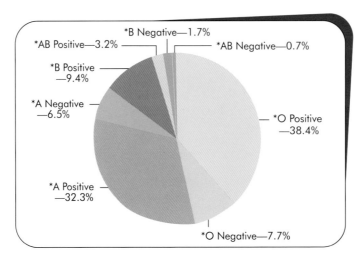

Most Americans have O+ blood, according to these figures from the American Red Cross.

*B Negative—1.7%
*AB Positive—3.2%
*AB Negative—0.7%
*B Positive —9.4%
*A Negative —6.5%
*O Positive —38.4%
*A Positive —32.3%
*O Negative—7.7%

18

Blood and crime

Traces of blood left at a crime scene can provide valuable information. The shape of blood drops can show the height from which the drops fell and the direction from which they came. A special type of light called **ultraviolet light** can be used to show where blood stains have been washed away from a piece of clothing or furniture.

A person who studies blood is called a serologist. Serologists analyze even the smallest traces of blood found at the scene. They can work out what blood type the person has, whether they had been drinking alcohol or taking drugs, and sometimes they can tell if the person had a disease.

You might find blood at a crime scene that is the same blood type as your suspect. But this does not prove that the suspect was there. Many people have the same blood types, so it only proves that someone with the same blood type as the suspect was there. This adds to the body of evidence, which may help to find a criminal or clear a suspect, but it is not **conclusive** evidence. Forensic scientists no longer determine the blood type found at the crime scene. They now use a new technique called DNA profiling that can use many different types of samples from a person (such as skin, hair or **saliva**) to match with a suspect.

Serologists often have only a small sample of blood to work with.

What is DNA profiling?

People have DNA in just about every cell in their bodies. DNA is the material that contains the information that makes you who you are. Everybody has different DNA (except identical twins). DNA makes every person look different than everyone else.

When forensic scientists find the tiniest part of a person like a strand of hair, a drop of blood, a flake of skin or even some saliva left on chewing gum, they can analyze the DNA and work out exactly who it came from. This process is called DNA profiling. DNA profiling is the most important breakthrough in forensic science since the discovery of fingerprints. It is sometimes called DNA fingerprinting.

The shape of a DNA molecule is called a double helix.

This person is setting up the equipment for a DNA profile.

What is DNA?

DNA stands for **d**eoxyribo**n**ucleic **a**cid. DNA is a very complicated **molecule** that contains all the **genetic** information needed to build a living thing. It is carried in tiny structures called chromosomes, found in your cells. You inherit your DNA from both your parents, and you will pass some of it on to your children. Because every person is different, every person has different DNA. But the DNA in every different cell in every part of your body is exactly the same.

Making a DNA profile

Only a tiny amount of DNA is needed to make a profile. Scientists can make copies of the DNA sample until they have enough to work with. Once they have enough copies they mix the DNA molecules with other molecules called enzymes, which cut up the DNA in particular places. The sample is now a mixture of DNA pieces of different sizes. The number and size of the pieces are different for every person.

The DNA pieces are then put onto a special jelly. Electricity is passed through the jelly, which causes the pieces to spread out into a pattern that looks a bit like a bar code. The smaller pieces move more quickly through the jelly than the larger pieces. The pattern is then compared to the pattern made by the suspect's or victim's sample. If the positions of the bands match up then it is extremely likely that the samples are from the same person.

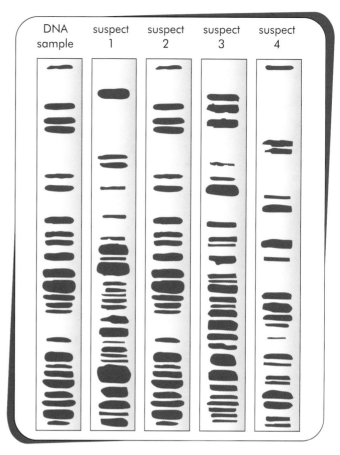

Can you see which suspect matches the sample?

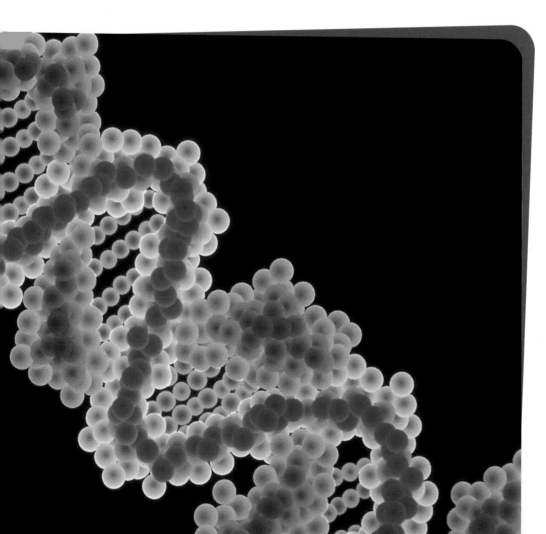

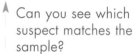

Science fact

Solving crimes from the past

Forensic scientists were able to use DNA profiling to identify bones from a person who had drowned 13 years earlier. They did this by matching the DNA with the dead man's son. The bones belonged to a man named Josef Mengele, who was responsible for the deaths of many hundreds of people in Poland during World War II.

Clues in your cleaning up

↑ The microscope shows that this hair has fallen out.

↑ This hair has been pulled out.

Have you ever thought about what makes up the dust around your house? Most of it is flakes of dead skin. You lose between 30,000 and 40,000 dead skin cells every minute. You also lose about 70 head hairs every day and they can end up in the dust along with bits of fluff and fibers from your clothes and furniture. Soil comes in on your shoes. All of these things can provide valuable clues about who has been in your house and when.

Crime investigators often sweep up dust to find evidence at a crime scene. They even check the dust inside people's vacuum cleaners. They can often find tiny particles of soil or hairs or fibers that link a suspect to a crime.

Hair

When you look at the people around you, it is easy to see that everyone has different hair. All hair is made mainly from a tough **protein** called keratin. Your nails are also made of keratin. Although everyone's hair is made from keratin, if you examine the hairs under a microscope, they are different. Hairs have different colors. Some people have fine hair, and others have thick, coarse hair. Some hairs are round, while others are flat. Forensic scientists can tell where on your body a hair came from. They can analyze the hair and find out what type of shampoo or hair coloring you have been using. They can even find out information about what you have been eating!

Science term

Proteins are a group of chemicals found in all living things.

Weird science

In 1960 a team of forensic scientists analyzed a hair sample from the famous French leader Napoleon Bonaparte, who had died in 1821. There had been many rumors about how he died. Special scientists (now called toxicologists) found that the level of the element arsenic was 13 times higher than normal. Arsenic is poisonous, and in those days it was used to make paint and wallpaper. They believed that Napoleon absorbed the poison by touching the walls, and it eventually killed him.

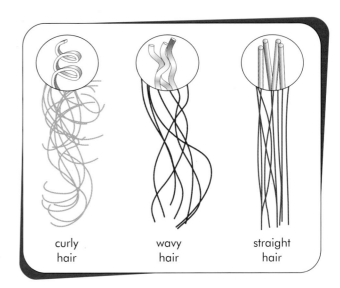

Curly, wavy and straight hair have different structures.

curly hair

wavy hair

straight hair

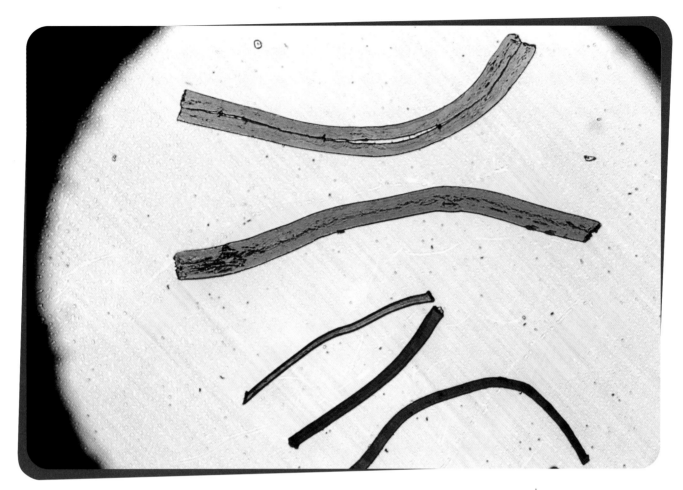

These fibers are all blue, but they are not from the same type of material.

Fibers

Fibers are loose threads from clothing and furniture. You might find fibers at the crime scene or in a suspect's house or car. Although fibers may look alike to the naked eye, under the microscope they look quite different. You can tell whether the fiber is natural, like cotton or wool, or whether it is **synthetic**, like nylon or polyester. You can also tell whether the fibers have been stretched, torn or cut. Comparison microscopes are used to carefully match fibers found at the crime scene.

Soil

Different places can have different soil types. Geologists, who study soil and rocks, can trace soil to exactly where it came from. Scientists look for soil on the soles of shoes, in carpet, under fingernails, on tires and in cars. Soil can be easily carried from one place to another on clothing, skin, shoes and in cars. If the soil found on or near a body does not match the soil type where the body is found, then it is likely that the body was moved. Geologists use microscopes to examine the color and shape of the soil particles, and chemical analysis to work out exactly what it is made of.

Science fact

Some clues are rubbish

Trash bins are searched by investigators trying to solve crimes. They may find a letter that has been thrown away and might be able to identify the handwriting. A bus ticket might tell them where someone has been. They might find fingerprints on a takeout food container. The saliva left on a piece of chewing gum can be used for DNA profiling to find out who was chewing the gum!

Have you ever been to the dentist and seen the charts that they use to keep a record of your teeth? The dentist marks where you have had fillings and if any teeth have been removed. Often dentists take x rays of your mouth to see if your teeth are too crowded or if you have a cavity. If you have braces or a dental plate, the dentist sometimes takes an impression of your teeth and makes a plaster model of your mouth.

These charts, x rays and models, along with notes made by the dentist, are your dental record. Everyone has quite different teeth patterns, which can be as useful as fingerprints and blood types in linking a suspect with a crime.

Tough teeth

Teeth last longer than any other part of your body. Adults usually have 32 **permanent** teeth that are designed to last a lifetime. They are covered in a white or yellowish substance called enamel. Enamel is the hardest substance in your body. Teeth are almost impossible to destroy. Teeth can be damaged, however, by mouth acid, which may build up in your mouth when bacteria and old food react together.

A full mouth x ray tells the dentist a lot about your teeth.

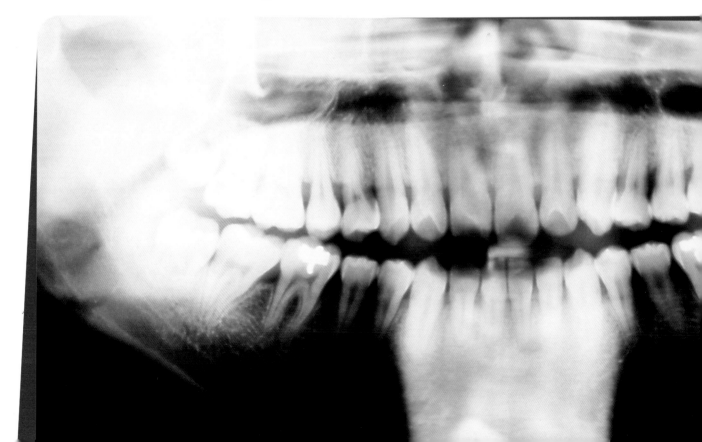

Identifying teeth and lips

Forensic odontologists are dentists who specialize in matching teeth to bite marks and identifying bodies by their teeth. People leave bite marks in all sorts of things including foam drinking cups, pencils, chewing gum and all sorts of food. Because teeth last for so long, forensic odontologists can often identify badly burned bodies by comparing the victim's teeth with dental records.

Just like your teeth pattern, the ridges on your lips are also unique. People often leave lip prints on cups and glasses. A person can be identified by their lip prints in much the same way as they can be identified by their fingerprints. Lipstick left behind can be chemically analyzed and compared to a suspect's lipstick.

Lipstick makes a mark that is easy to see.

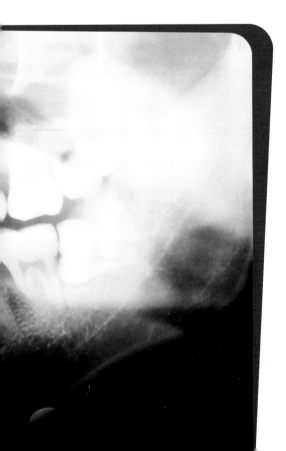

You leave teeth marks in all sorts of places.

Science fact

Teeth marks can bite you back

A forensic odontologist in London once identified the driver of a getaway car from the bite mark he left in a plastic key tag. A murderer was identified from the bite marks left in a half-eaten pear at the scene of the crime.

25

Paper and ink

Handwriting

Everyone's handwriting is different. Your teacher could probably recognize your writing, even if your name was missing from your work. A handwritten note can provide a lot of evidence. Handwriting can be analyzed by handwriting experts, and the paper and ink can be analyzed chemically.

Handwriting can give information about the likely age of the person who wrote a note. Handwriting experts carefully examine the shape of each letter, the spacing of each letter, its slope, any special pen strokes or decoration, and how each letter is formed. They also look at whether lowercase or capital letters are used, the position of the cross on a 't' or the dot on an 'i'. The back of the paper may also be checked to see how heavily the writer's pen pushed into the paper.

Chromatography

Scientists use chromatography to identify many different chemicals, including inks. Most inks are made up of a number of different colors, called pigments, mixed together. For example, the black ink in a ballpoint pen may be made up from blue, red and yellow ink. The ink in another brand of black ballpoint pen will probably be made up from a different combination of colors.

Chromatography separates the inks into their different colors and can identify the type of pen used to write a note or sign a document. Chemists also use chromatography to analyze mystery powders and liquids found at crime scenes.

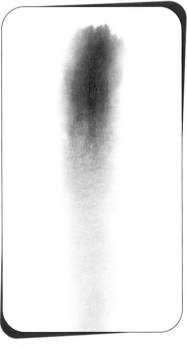

Chromatography shows that inks are made of many different colors.

Look carefully at these two different samples of handwriting. Which writer do you think was older?

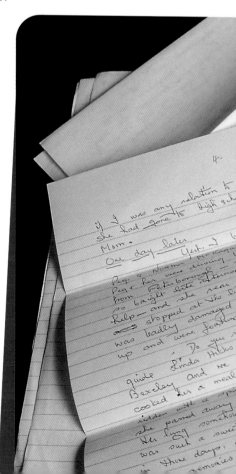

Infrared luminescence

Forgery is a serious crime. Forgers try to copy or change important legal papers, checks and even paper money. For example, forgers might try to print or write over the original amount written on a check. Forensic scientists can look at the check under special blue light, which shows up some kinds of ink but not others. If the amount on the check has been changed using a different brand of pen, one type of ink can absorb the blue light and become excited. This is called luminescence. The excited ink then gives off a special type of light, called infrared light, which shows up in a special television screen. The other ink does not show up, so the forgery can easily be seen.

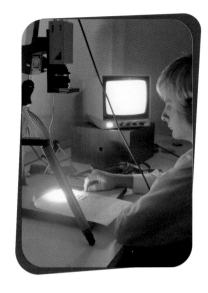

▲ This person is examining some documents using infrared luminescence.

Paper

There are many different sorts of paper. Toilet paper is different from writing paper. Recycled paper is made from other waste paper. Some paper is made from cotton or flax plants. Paper is usually made from wood fibers. Wood is mushed into a pulp, mixed with different chemicals, and then dried and rolled. Chemicals are sometimes added to make paper whiter or shinier or stronger.

Forensic scientists are able to analyze the type of paper found at a crime scene. They look at the tear pattern and the shape and length of the fibers in the paper. They can match paper from the crime scene with paper owned by a suspect.

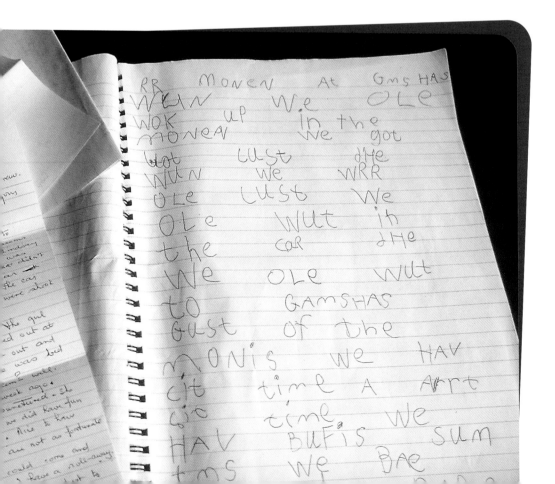

Autopsies

Many crimes involve someone dying. A specially trained doctor, called a forensic pathologist, will go to the scene of a suspicious death. They do this so that they can look at the dead body in the place where it was found. This can often give them clues about how the person died. When the body is removed, it is taken to a place called a mortuary. The forensic pathologist may perform an autopsy (or post-mortem), which is an examination of the body to help to find out the cause of the death. It involves examining the outside of the body as well as the inside. The body is checked for diseases, injuries, and the presence of poisons or drugs.

Time of death

Temperature

After somebody dies, their body temperature starts to fall. The longer a person has been dead, the lower their temperature becomes. Their body temperature will also depend on the weather conditions and temperature at the crime scene.

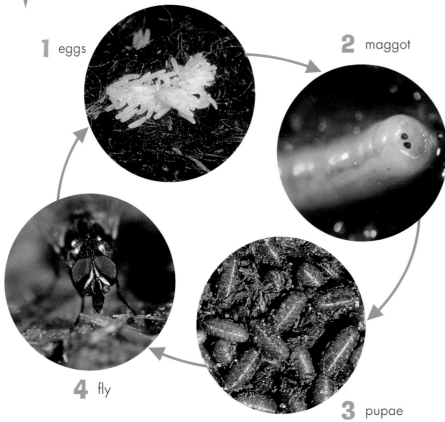

The life cycle of a fly has four different stages.

1 eggs

2 maggot

4 fly

3 pupae

Flies

Some flies lay their eggs in dead bodies. After a short time, each egg hatches into a grub called a maggot. The maggot then forms a case around itself and turns into a **pupa**. After a while, the adult fly breaks out of the case. Together these stages form the life cycle of a fly.

A scientist who studies insects is called an entomologist. Forensic entomologists have studied the life cycles of different sorts of flies. They know exactly how long each stage takes, and so they can estimate how long a person has been dead.

Meet a forensic technician

Have you ever asked yourself what it would be like to be a forensic scientist? What sorts of jobs are there? How is it possible to get a job? What do you have to study in high school and at college?

Meet Carolyn de Koenig

Carolyn de Koenig has the answers to these questions. She is a forensic technician. She helps to find out how and why some people die.

Carolyn became interested in science because it gave her answers to some of her questions about the world. At school she studied science and then completed a science degree at college.

Carolyn de Koenig.

Carolyn works with doctors called forensic pathologists who look closely at a dead person's body to see if there are any diseases or injuries that may have caused death. Her job is similar to that of a nurse in an operating room, except that she performs some parts of the operation. She also takes x rays and makes sure the samples the pathologist has taken reach the laboratory safely.

Carolyn wanted to be involved in this kind of work because it helps to answer people's questions about friends and family who have died.

Carolyn says that if you want a career as a forensic pathologist you must be prepared to study hard. You need a strong stomach too because sometimes you see some awful things. When you are old enough you could think about doing work experience in a hospital or even with a funeral director to see what a career in this field might be like.

Forensic science timeline

This timeline shows some important forensic science events. See if you can imagine some of the things that might happen in forensic science in the future.

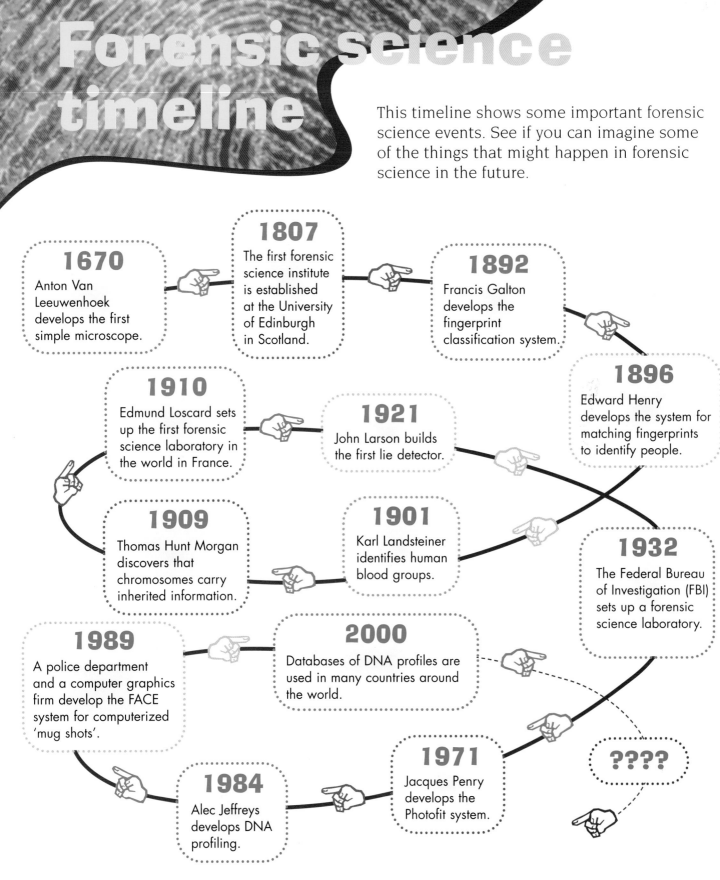

1670
Anton Van Leeuwenhoek develops the first simple microscope.

1807
The first forensic science institute is established at the University of Edinburgh in Scotland.

1892
Francis Galton develops the fingerprint classification system.

1896
Edward Henry develops the system for matching fingerprints to identify people.

1910
Edmund Loscard sets up the first forensic science laboratory in the world in France.

1921
John Larson builds the first lie detector.

1909
Thomas Hunt Morgan discovers that chromosomes carry inherited information.

1901
Karl Landsteiner identifies human blood groups.

1932
The Federal Bureau of Investigation (FBI) sets up a forensic science laboratory.

1989
A police department and a computer graphics firm develop the FACE system for computerized 'mug shots'.

2000
Databases of DNA profiles are used in many countries around the world.

????

1971
Jacques Penry develops the Photofit system.

1984
Alec Jeffreys develops DNA profiling.

What are scientists working on now?

⊙ Scientists have found a way of telling different paper samples apart using a chemical fingerprinting technique called mass spectrometry.

Glossary

bacteria microscopic living organisms (When there is one it is called a bacterium.)

conclusive without a doubt

electrons tiny, negatively charged particles

genetic having to do with the way your characteristics are inherited

molecule a group of atoms that are chemically bonded together

permanent long-lasting

protein a group of chemicals found in all living things

pupa the third stage in an insect's life, after the egg and larvae

reconstruct to build again

saliva digestive juices in your mouth

synthetic something made or manufactured by humans and not naturally occurring

ultraviolet light high-energy light that is invisible to the human eye

Index